TO: BRI

MW01075068

I wrote so many of
these pages in your
home. Thank you for
being my family.
♡ Krista

this will set me free

this will set me free

KRISTIN MICHELLE ELIZABETH

BROOKLYN, NY

Copyright © 2017 by Kristin Michelle Elizabeth. All rights reserved.

Cover design by KJ Parish.

Published by Thought Catalog Books, a publishing house owned by The Thought & Expression Co., Williamsburg, Brooklyn.

First edition, 2017

ISBN: 978-1945796692

Printed and bound in the United States.

10 9 8 7 6 5 4 3 2 1

I am too much
put me back on the shelf

and I say that because
I am too much
for even myself

I am the book
you always opened
but never read

I am the song
you always played
but you never listened
to the lyrics

you were too focused
on the beat

this is for anyone
who knows how it feels
to feel like me

free

free

frē/

adjective

1. not under the control or in the power of another; able to act or be done as one wishes.
2. not physically restrained, obstructed, or fixed; unimpeded.

verb

1. release from captivity, confinement, or slavery.

"free." New Oxford American Dictionary. Oxford University Press, 2011. Web. 22 Aug 2017.

eye of the storm

a never-ending, manic frenzy
consumes me

a restless, electric energy
that refuses to be still

I feel suffocated
in this apartment
trapped in my own head

my inner voice
is always screaming at me

I am so filled with emotion

when the tide is high
the waves of my soul
come crashing down

wipe me out and anyone else
that stands too close
to my personal shore

I grew up dancing in the rain
when I am sad, I do not cry
I bawl rainstorms

I have a heart of thunder
lightning in my veins

mind destructive, quick
like a tornado

brooding darkness
always leads to a light
at the end of the tunnel

I remind myself
the storm will calm
as I dance around
in the funnel

even if only
for a short period of time
until it riles me up again

weathering my natural disaster
I am my own spiritual master

a chaotic whirlwind surrounds me
dizzying myself

I dance in the eye of my hurricane
and hope the gusts
that follow me around

only touch bystanders enough
to remind them that
they are *alive*

broken

bro·ken

ˈbrō kən

adjective

1. (of a person) having given up all hope; despairing.
2. having been fractured or damaged and no longer in one piece or in working order.
3. having breaks or gaps in continuity.

"broken." New Oxford American Dictionary. Oxford University Press, 2011.Web. 22 Aug 2017.

island blues

I'm longing for a familiar face
the only home I know
is a nostalgic place

I cannot see or hear anything
but you

the echoes of our gasps for air
used to be music to my ears

now nausea fills the room
as these memories of doom
fully consume

we'll never be reasonable
with our wants and dares
unattainable and illogical
with animal-like behaviors

it's always,
this is the last time, I swear...

it's hard to get a point across
when in your own head
you're lost

deep down I know you'll leave
and I'll keep reminding myself
to breathe

the sun sets in the winter
I feel mentally sicker

sand, sweat, and laughter
bruised and naked
it's always been me you're after

appreciating the beauty of the sunset
knowing this is the best
it is ever going to get

you'll ask,
remember what you said to me
I'll shake my head 'no'
cautiously

words are only words
and my alter ego
is a free bird

I say what I mean
then forget and pretend
it was only a dream

I'll never be yours
you'll never be mine
but you know how
to control my mind

the beauty is you'll flee
and I just want to be free

forever singing,
please don't forget me...

love is hard

if it were easy
for me to communicate
I would not be writing this

if you could read my mind
you would know
it is a dark abyss

if love were easy you would know
you have had me from the start
confusion consumes my being
when we are apart

if love were easy
I would be better at this
I would be able to tell you
how much I long for your kiss

your wit, humor, and zest for life
our similarities that result in strife

your messy hair, your piercing eyes
the way I tremble when you're
between my thighs

the way you smoke your cigarette
the way you push back your hair
I was always the fool
who could not help but stare

if love were easy
we would always agree
we would never get angry
we would not be you and me

if it were easy
love would always be fun
you would put me back together
when I so frequently come undone

if love were easy
we would never grow
I wouldn't feel this low
because you would just know

toxic attraction

I feel everything
your joy, your pain
your weakness

the first time
you fantasized about
going underneath my blankets

most say I am crazy
I tend to be lazy

takes twelve hours
to get out of bed

little do you know
everything you said
is stuck inside of my head

my heart beats fast
I believe things will last

it is wishful thinking
believing you understand me
has me sinking

I can't make you want to
relate to my past
you quickly remind me
how I am like your last

it can be a bitter pattern
of who is right or wrong
for only the ego
will sing this song

there is a fine line to be drawn
between feeling and reason
for without feeling
what would humans believe in

remember this the next time
your ego wants to attack
I've come to find...
you do not have my back

poetic chaos

terrified to pick up a pen
because the truth will flow
out of my fingertips

yet this is the only way
I can find my inner zen

your departure

home base
a constant reminder
of the company I used to keep
in this space

but you were so far-flung
it's like you were never here
at all

you fled
just like the others
I told you about
while we argued in bed

I am completely content
with not begging anyone
to stay

if they never wanted to be here
in the first place

sadness disease

woke up with a headache
blurry vision
my heart aches
a cloudy mind
an innate sadness
please today
be kind

betrayal

who do you turn to
when the one you used to turn to
turns on you too

doused

tell them the truth
tell them I was the fire
that kept you warm

tell them
the fear of getting burned
terrified you

so you put out my flame
turned me cold and blue
like you

ghost

you'll never stop missing me
my voice will haunt
in the echoes of the wind
and in the waves of the sea
that lick the shore
because in hopes of a brighter future
I tend to give my soul
which in time
becomes irreplaceable

incomparable

my name
will come to your lips
as you grab on to
her desperate hips

you will search for me
inside of her

just to find
no one compares

return to sender

if you truly cared
about my well-being
you'd keep your thoughts
to yourself

you'd let me go
like I asked you to

if you truly loved me
you wouldn't feel the need
to justify your actions
or remind me of words
I said in the past

if you were sincere
your letters
would not only be about you

you would ask
how I was doing too

too late

you only want me now
because you realize
what you had

selfish lovers
only want love
once it is too late
and the damage is done

selfless lovers
do anything at the time
to keep their partner happy

and that is why
there is no coming back
you were not there
when I was

and now
you are too late

repercussions

I am not the type of woman
who gives up

I see potential
and try to get you to bend
into a better version of yourself
overextending myself

I am too much you say
too passionate, too aware
too driven, yet too aloof
with an intense stare

you have to love yourself first
for who you are
before a woman like me
could ever set the bar

when asked how I moved forward
so easily

vivid memories come in flashes

I am **broken** on the ground
unhappy

dead inside

I was always a ghost
do not act
as if this is news to you
that is why this ended
in the first place

but this time
I am not around
and it's haunting you

because you know
you never listened
when I told you
what was killing me inside

love can make you blind

the only time I felt alive
was when you physically got me
out of my mind

and I had no choice
other than to feel

but this is not on you
I was dead when you found me

...I think I killed you too

the remedy

rem·e·dy

ˈre mə dē/

noun

1. a medicine or treatment for a disease or injury.
2. a means of counteracting or eliminating something undesirable.

"remedy." New Oxford American Dictionary. Oxford University Press, 2011.Web. 22 Aug 2017.

fire and air

he walks into the room
radiant energy
consumes my being

the type of energy you feel
while you pretend
you're not looking

cool, calm, and collected
yet a hungry stare
this type of company
is incredibly rare

a human who proceeds with caution
to protect his heart
who won't ruin his status
for a false jump start

maturity and strength
more present
than impulsive energy
conversation and understanding
lead to an undeniable synergy

an intellectual, passionate
self-caring man
how stupid I would be
if I took his vigilance personal
and ran

your ocean

I either have a case of word vomit
or I'm unable say a thing

forever wondering
why I love so much
but show so little

I want to believe in this rush
but when my guard comes down
anxiety consumes me

reminding me I could drown
in your ocean
as if you secretly slipped me
love potion

so I keep you at arm's length
because the only loyalty I know
is my own inner strength

I should know by now
that when I try to avoid
I fall in deep, I never sleep

wake me up from this dream
I can't even blink
I'll ride this wave
until I sink

losing sleep

my imagination lingers
to thoughts of your striking face
I'm running a race
and feel as if I am in first place

but your silences
have me second guessing
could this be love or another lesson

you consume me
I feel crazy

why can't I get you
off of my mind

is love truly this blind
or are we lying to ourselves
to maintain a balanced state of mind

your smile lights up my day
I always have too much to say

I can't shut up my stupid mouth
I leave your place
consumed with doubt

I can't stop drinking
because every time I try
reality hits

as I imagine
the taste of your lips
and the grip you could have
on my hips

I care so much about you
so I ignore my thoughts
until it is late
and I connect the dots

I will not say another word
until the timing is right

I want to love you
like no one has loved you before
nothing scares me anymore
but am I the one you truly adore

this is all in my head
I've been losing sleep
tossing and turning in bed

patience

I must learn patience
and to take my time
how fortunate am I
to have gotten closer to someone
who can make me rhyme

we melt into his couch
all I can think about
are his hands and mouth

we don't touch
I say too much

I pull my coat hood
over my head
as my cheeks turn
rosy red

my lust is strong
when I don't see him
I long

placebo

forever pretending
I am mistaking
salt for sugar

I know you are salty
I will make you sweet
or at least pretend to

words he'll never say

she has James Dean
tattooed on her side
she only drinks
cheap red wine

she likes to walk
in the pouring rain
those who misunderstand her
call her insane

she is quirky and fierce
with dark eyes that pierce

she beckons the angel and devil
on her shoulder
she dismisses those who are toxic
as she grows older

she's a fiery mess
I can't stop thinking about her
she's unlike the rest

she writes poems
and tries to turn them into songs
she helps me write off
all of my wrongs

she buzzes with ideas
right after the world's gone to sleep

she's my favorite little secret
I plan to keep

clean slate

you once gave your soul
lost control

learned in the end
all those times you had to bend

only lead you
to putting yourself back together

wondering why love
never lasts forever

you are scared to open up
your heart is fragile
let it mend

I wish you knew
how much I relate
all I know is heartbreak

but what if we met
with a clean slate

rebel

he asks, why me
as he pours us hot tea

my hands are drawn to his body
my lips to his skin

I get so tongue tied
lying next to him

I used to think he was cold
but his hidden warmth
has me sold

he's nervous
he can't sit still
by now I know the drill

hide your feelings
play cool

don't fall in love
don't be a fool

I've always been a rebel
when it comes to romance

he's worth the risk

...I take the chance

chaos

cha·os

ˈkā äs

noun

1. complete disorder and confusion.

PHYSICS

1. behavior so unpredictable as to appear random, owing to great sensitivity to small changes in conditions.
2. the formless matter supposed to have existed before the creation of the universe.

"chaos." New Oxford American Dictionary. Oxford University Press, 2011.Web. 22 Aug 2017.

consequences

your hands are like an ocean
drowning my mind

tangled in one another
your lips on mine

both aware
of the impending darkness
that will follow momentary bliss

craving the lights to be on
so this is real

I felt you escape to a place
where your heart remained closed
fearfully pushing me away
past memories consuming you
relating me to her

I knew
there was nothing I could do
to change your mind

so I left that day
knowing you got what you want
but not what you need

dreaming of a future
where love wins and pride dies

when reality hits

what can I do
am I in love with you
or the thought of you

you tell me exactly
what you think and mean

but I am blinded
because the in-betweens
make me realize
it is never as it seems

drowning

I'm not the type of woman
to expect flowers or a public post
but I crave to know
you adore me most

you don't have to say the words
you don't have to try
our energy speaks so loud
I know that love is you and I

you will always be enough for me
I wish you could see what I see
you bring me to my knees

I want all that is not mine
you are one of the only
who can make me rhyme

you don't know how to love
yet you're an angel
sent from above

I can't help but wonder
how your tide
pulled me under

waves

I am in my head
thoughts of me naked
in your bed

how did your hand
turn a fire like me
into an ocean

you asked,
do you get that wet for everyone

filled with emotion
I only let another touch me
if they look inside and see

please get out of my head
I'm not sure if it is you
or the thought of love
that I dread

counterfeit romance

you say,
we have too much in common
it tends to make you run

you had me at the bottom
of your abyss
before we even kissed

I see the pain in your eyes
I feel the hesitance
as you tiptoe around me
did I not make you feel alive

you used to wrap yourself around me
so tightly

blurry lines
tend to be infinite
I am so over it

this cannot be real
if all you have learned
is how to hide what you feel

it's not you, it's me

he asks,
why do you continue to write about me

ah, it's not you
it's the thought of what you could be
and only that has the power
for others to be able to relate
to a girl like me

rather let you slip away

you were my type
but I'm so over the hype

I no longer want someone
who would rather be right
than be by my side

I write poems, I'm too deep
doesn't mean you're someone
I'm trying to keep

I will not chase anyone
who acts like we are done
before it has even begun

I have been that woman before
I have nothing to hide anymore
diminishing my self-worth for love
teaches my soul how to soar

I'd rather let you slip away
than try to convince you
why you should come my way

unrequited

I love him
I wish he loved himself
so he can love me too

desire

you said,
don't wait for me

I'm not waiting
but I'm also not leaving

I care about you
I am so flustered
my white flag is up

you want someone unlike me
yet your actions align
with my dreams

I only think romantically
about you
I have been feeling
so blue

I can fit any mold
if it is for you
the one
I long to hold

ignorance

I exclaimed,
you cannot hurt me

there I go again
with my stupid pride
found myself later
lying by your side

torn apart
by a wolf in a mask
how ignorant was I
to think this would last

fantasist

our love was not real
seemed to only be in my head

yet I continue to idolize you
fall for you
think of you in bed

the dark circles
beneath my brown eyes
tell the truth
I so desperately hide

I am a dreamer
such a lush

when memories come back
they come in flashes
and I never know if they are real
or if I made them up

beggars cannot be choosers

in the end
we will both lose
the universe hands us love
and we try to dismiss the feeling

pick and choose
another distraction
to use and abuse

you want someone
who can calm you down
who is not like me

I am too much of a fire
to be the one you desire

shake you up, make you crazy
your nonsensical love
makes me lazy

yet here I stand
wanting to be in your company
because you looked inside
understood the roller coaster ride
of my emotional, chaotic side

I want you because you know
what it feels like to be like me

but in the end
this is only going to kill me

cannot have your cake and eat it too

do not resent me
you were the one who did not want me
in the first place

I feel no need to censor myself
at the convenience of your comfort zone
throw me no more bones

this is not a race
time for me to save face
you simply get what you give

I only ever wanted you
now here we are
moving on, forgetting you

lights out

I'll dim my shine for you
but only if it means
you can breathe again

chemical reaction

fire cannot exist without air
the more air on offer
the brighter the flame burns

air stifles as fire ignites
but do not forget
hot air rises

...float away, my friend

the demons inside

de·mon

ˈdē mən

noun

1. an evil spirit or devil, especially one thought to possess a person or act as a tormentor in hell.

    - a cruel, evil, or destructive person or thing.
    - a forceful, fierce, or skillful performer of a specified activity.
    - reckless mischief; devilry.

"demon." New Oxford American Dictionary. Oxford University Press, 2011.Web. 22 Aug 2017.

damsel in distress

the lightning within me
will not allow me to ignore
the rhythm of my anxiety

I avoided destruction
focused on a distraction
just to face this bottomless hole
months later

this time the pain has doubled
but I'm not the only one
who is truly troubled

joke's on me

I cannot help but wonder
why you didn't say goodbye
my heart is filled with thunder

it's either
you'll see me in the future
or my suffering has become
your latest humour

runaways

I no longer take others'
leave of absence personally
for it has nothing to do
with me

running away
does not cure anxiety

running prolongs the truth
from slapping you in the face
all of my cards on the table now
here is my ace

I ran away once
I dealt with the aftermath
for months

I know by now
that when I try to avoid
reality catches up
haunts and destroys

memories make you feel sick
you begin to question,
what could I have done
to make this outcome different

my heart breaks but I don't
throw me no more bones

the only way out of your head
is to pump the breaks and deal
actions take precedence
over words once said

face emotions
listen to your heart
ego is the only force
tearing love and connection
apart

I finally know
the answer is not you
I hope you are able to find peace too

stomach this

I pick apart my food
so you pick apart me
remind me that
I am way too skinny

do you know what it's like
to not be able to stomach
your favorite food

because everything
makes you feel sick

my depression
does not have an appetite

every time you mention
I am underweight, I suffer
as if I was not already aware
of my deterioration

I am the one
who has to live with myself
every single day

underweight or overweight
what's it to you

it's not your responsibility
to judge or hate on

another's battle
within themselves

background noise

I am the album
you always played
but never listened to

simply there
for your convenience
so you can fall asleep at night

monster under my bed

his apologies
made me believe
it was my fault
that it was not assault

I cannot stand how irate
this makes me

this type of monster
must be stopped

no means no

I once woke up in hands
who took my body
as their own property
who would not take no
for an answer

who knew sleeping
on a trusted couch
could lead to such destruction

I am panicking
remembering the shrill of my inner voice
hysterically screaming,
get off of me right now

the sound of his voice saying,
but it feels so good
is haunting me
following me around

the worst part is he is someone
others consider a good friend
reality being
he is a disgusting foe

a thief
who stole a part of me
I wasn't willing to give

who is the reason I flinch
at the touch of a sincere hand

but he
will not ruin me

flashback to hell

in the blink of an eye
I am reminded of the feeling
that makes me want to die

this type of destruction
cannot be undone
all I can do is come to terms
with the situation

this was not a nightmare
even if the amount of booze
in my system
knocked me into delusion

the next day
I woke up at 3 p.m.
in a windowless room
with my bottoms
turned inside out
around my ankles

reminding me
how I desperately tried
to protect myself
while I pulled them up
between his murmurs
as he made his way
inside of me

he came into the room
shortly after I woke
offered me a drink and said,
I'm sorry

as if that
was going to erase this
from my memory

haunted

how he stepped foot
into my house again
is beyond me

but he did
while I was there

I locked myself in my room
the moment I heard his voice
I found my knees at my chin
while tears streamed down my face

I hid under my comforter
afraid of reliving his destruction

or worse
having to explain to everyone
why I was so distant

I became a ghost
in my own house

and by house
I don't mean just the structure
I grew up in

...but my own flesh too

phantom

if you run
from what scares you

don't be alarmed
when you see a ghost

revolution

rev·o·lu·tion

re və ˈloo shən

noun

1. a forcible overthrow of a government or social order in favor of a new system.
2. an instance of revolving.

- the movement of an object in a circular or elliptical course around another or about an axis or center.
- a single orbit of one object around another or about an axis or center.

"revolution." New Oxford American Dictionary. Oxford University Press, 2011.Web. 22 Aug 2017.

fuel

there is a fire within me
I could burn you to the ground

I'll turn this energy into fuel
and ignite myself

while I leave you in the smoke

because if you were meant
to be in my life

you would have never
lit the match

if your intention was to let
the flame burn out

pyromaniac

she is sharp
with a witty tongue
that tends to get her in trouble

she has no issue
with burning a bridge
and watching it go up in flames
if it means staying true to herself

she makes worlds spin
while standing still

she is the spark that starts fires
she is the spirit that remains
when the fire fizzles out

after dark

you will hear my song
on the radio
read my thoughts
on your news feed
see my face
in all of your dreams

those closest to you
will give you grief for losing me
what is reality?

you buried me so deep
the thought of my love
makes you sick

sent me away
from your conscious

that when you least expect it
my face will appear
and it will hurt you
as much as you hurt me

and I will make fame
out of the pain you cause

while you suffer
and regret what you did
for the rest of your life

fair-weather friends

no more giving the upper-hand
to those who reprimand
before they listen to understand

no more giving the best parts
of myself
to those who carelessly handle
my heart

they say people do not change
but watch me rearrange

I will never allow
my tender, thoughtful heart
to be stepped on again
by those who tear me down
yet consider themselves
a good friend

if you were true
you would be next to me
helping me through the blue

tired

do not mistake
my kindness for weakness

I am kind
but I am no tool
I know what I am doing
forever flattering the fool

I am always on time
you are always late
I'll leave it to karma
to handle your fate

I advise you to pay attention
to your conscience
it will haunt you
if ignored

be careful
who you push aside
it is the same ole story
and I am so bored

forget you

hate me for who I was to you
forget the good I do

hate me for the illusion
your mind drew

but verbalize my authenticity
as anything but true

and watch the rest of your life
be painted blue

louder

I was always
the lyrical tune in your ear
turned up too loud

you always had a way
of turning me down

It's time my beat drowns you *out*

funk that

mix-tapes and love
are one in the same for me

I don't play or tune into it
unless I'm feeling it

acceptance

holding on
to whatever feeling I find
puts me in a bind

torn between who I am
and who I want to be

trying to accept the fact
I was born crazy

bona fide

she speaks articulately
and writes thoughtfully

she says what is on her mind
and kindly dismisses anyone
that doesn't favor her authenticity

sunshine

a mind that never sits still
although quiet
her stare could kill

unapproachable and reserved
she focuses on individuals
whose attention is deserved

an influential force that fights for change
her demeanors are perceived by most
as strange

hair that falls below her breasts
wavy and frazzled
she can be such a mess

an optimist at heart
she's called sunshine
by those who understand
she is a work of art

the hardest lesson

I cannot help you
If I do not learn
how to help myself first

a dog's love

sincere, loyal
forgiving, unwavering
beyond true

a guiding light
to help me out of the blue

by my side
through thick and thin
good and sin

Simba,
the light of my life
I am so very lucky to call you
my best friend

convenience

I am the woman you pass
on the street

my energy
catches your attention

we lock eyes so intensely
but I do not even notice
you are there

I am in my own inner world
lost in my fantasies

your eyes are just convenient

outlier

she pushes her limits
shakes up the status quo
rips the envelope open
if she has to

no one can box her in
she will never conform
to be a part of a clique
that doesn't match her values

a rebel, a misfit, a freak of nature
she confuses those who color
inside of the lines

because she is free
her home is wherever
she wants it to be

true security
can only be found
within herself

inner voice

she follows her intuition
and trusts it's leading her
in the right direction

generalist

jack of all trades
master of none

but once you learn
how to juggle
you rarely drop the ball

on fire

I am always on fire
because being a perfectionist
is actual hell

cannot be tamed

the fire within me
cannot be put out
for long

only those who crave passion
can experience my inner lioness
life is not about
focusing on emptiness

I express my demons
just to remind myself
I am alive

forever craving adventure
human connection
wildness

ruthless

I am a fool
for what I want

I love the game
that I cannot win

no apologies

I lived my entire life saying sorry
when I was not in the wrong
to maintain the status quo
that woman is long gone

here I am
writing another song
out of the pain you cause

all you do
is point out my flaws

one day you will know
what it feels like
to feel like me

and I will not be around
to hear your plea

deal with your demons
I came to terms with mine

I was in the dark
for so long

now it's time
for my wings to soar
and my light to shine

guarded

I will never apologize
for trying to break down walls

that should have never been built
in the first place

harmony

if nothing else
music is safe

my outlet and joy
my escape
from a mundane reality

my way of connecting
to other humans

who know what it is like
to feel like me

stronger than yesterday

kicked me down
when I was already
on the ground

tread lightly
now that I am back up

a breath of fresh air

she asks,
are you trying to intimidate me
because if so it is working

he says,
depends
is it a good or bad thing
be careful what you wish for, my dear
it is a slippery slope

who said she was wishing

he laughs,
only time will tell
I want to see your dark side
you are so in your head
I would love to get you out of it

as he grabs
the shark tooth around her neck

she asks,
do you like sharks?

he sarcastically rolls his eyes,
if you did your research
you would know
I swim with them frequently
you are quite endearing

an Australian actor in her face
watching her drink boba tea
out of a straw
in a cafe

he is quite a beautiful man
why the hell is he pursuing her

watching her every move
his blue eyes are quite hypnotizing
his accent quite sexual

she probably won't see him again
no desire to

but he bites his lip and whispers,
you are so forward
you will see me again

she questions her existence
as she takes it all in

a man with flair
a breath of fresh air
a man to remind her
why the hell she is here

hard to get

first undress my mind
then maybe you can undress me
in time

this concept seems to be foreign
to so many

I don't want to be intimate
with just anybody

INFP

I lose energy
by human contact

moments alone
are essential to my well-being

even if your company
gives me pleasure

being extremely intuitive
can be quite the curse

why do I always know
before you do

here I go again
writing another verse

one lives a strange life
when they feel for others
more than they feel
for themselves

indefinite

I just keep going
it's like I'm in slow motion

I got a vision
I can't get out of my mind
you and me, that night
life can make you so blind

I had to know you
now I desire you
that electric feeling
when you walked in the room
I'll go insane if I don't see you soon

crazy laughter, city lights
drunk on wine, catching flights

we're all looking for love
in the strangest places
latching on to familiar faces

just call me Miley
I'm up to no good
I'd change my ways if I could

know it's a never-ending phase
I'm in a daze
always questioning my age

maybe one day it will all work out
until then I'll have my doubts

deity

I feel everyone's pain
I'm constantly in the rain

I ask the universe,
was I brought to this world
for reasons aside from myself

I answer my own question,
who am I to think
I can cure somebody else

awake

funny how the whole bad boy thing
can go from enticing to disgusting
in the blink of an enlightening moment

my prince charming

I am too much for most
too passionate, too emotional
too driven, too crazy
too complex

the one
will not have to try
to keep up with me
because he'll be right there
beside me
or a couple steps ahead
leading the way

our presence will set
this world on fire
as we ignite one another

past lovers
will hold their breath
as they whisper,

...that could have been me

ambitious

she has a passionate nature
an assertive manner

she comes off as aggressive
to those focused on
misunderstanding her

she knows what she wants
she works hard to obtain it

she has avenues to follow
goals to reach
she chases dreams like a cheetah
on the hunt

she does as she pleases
she does not want anyone to fix her
or hold her down

you are either on her side, by her side,
or in her *way*

rebirth

re·birth

rē 'bərth

noun

1. the process of being reincarnated or born again.
2. the action of reappearing or starting to flourish or increase after a decline; revival.

"rebirth." New Oxford American Dictionary. Oxford University Press, 2011.Web. 22 Aug 2017.

metamorphosis

only those who stick around
actually get to witness the caterpillar
turn into the butterfly

it's those whose eyes
were so fixated on the butterfly
they forgot the caterpillar existed
in the first place

I was hiding in my cocoon
for so long

I did not know wings
would come along with the darkness

...but you did

end of the rainbow

you can be
whoever you want to be
no matter what you are told

no one can stop you
from finding your pot of gold

when they asked what changed

I spent so much time
feeding others' hunger

I realized it is time
I start feeding mine

full moon

I ignored my thoughts
afraid I could not live up
to my truth

but those ocean eyes
seem to keep mine

I feel like a teenage girl
thrown off in a whirlwind
I must learn discipline

you've had my back
from the moment
I asked you to

what if
all of this time
true love is me and you

for the first time in my life
I am opening up my heart
to who and what
I deserve

the sun

you are my fire
the one who aspires to inspire

when the world kicks me down
you make me want to try even harder

even if I burn myself
in the process

alive

fantasy is reality
even if it is temporary
dreams are beyond ego

I would rather feel alive
than try to convince
a foolish mind

how to understand
a brain like mine

ethereal

you might as well be the sky
that twinkle in your eye

please don't stop looking at me
like that

you bring me right back
to life

power

I'll be your muse
as long as you're my fuse

starry-eyed

I miss the southern stars
so much

I cannot help but look at you
with that same amount
of lust

haiku

the moon and the stars
shine brighter than the city lights
you are on my mind

gravity

he asks,
how are you feeling
I want to ground you...

we laugh
because I was going to say
I feel like I am on Jupiter
about to take off for Pluto

but he already knows
his gravitational pull
is the reason

...I don't float away

grounded

the word grounded
always had a negative connotation
in my personal dictionary

that was until…
you came into my life

home

the air feels lighter
no wonder they call Los Angeles
the city of angels

the sky is lit
with pink and orange rays
a smile crosses my face
for the first time in days

in this moment
I discover my truth

It's *you*...
I'm finally back
to you

eclipse

me, the emotional moon
you, the vibrant sun
both of us more beautiful
when we are one

perseverance

I made a deal
with the stars
to keep going

to shine brightly
to help others
find their way home

when I die
I hope to be remembered
as the one who never gave up

who lived to ignite the flame
without the fear of getting burned

who saw the light in people
when they couldn't see it
within themselves

hidden depths

people will never recognize
what has changed within you…

what makes you tick
what sets your heart on fire
or what causes a rage within your bloodstream

unless they yearn to understand
your soul

hedonist

I have never suffered
from not knowing what I want

rather I want it all
at once

but the ones who suffer the most
do not know what they want
at all

puzzle solved

it's no longer a mystery
watch us go down in history

epilogue

to the fire
who illuminated the room
in my darkest times
a continuous light
selfless and true
thank you so much
for all that you do
please don't stop
taking the stage
you helped me through
every single page
your charisma reminds
people like me
to never stop fighting
for their dreams
you encourage me
to be the best I can be
to help others
who are hoping for a light
to shine on them
so they can finally see
the reflection of the human
they always aimed to be
thank you for being a hero
for helping me through the blue
for reminding me it's okay
to speak my truth
you are music to my ears

I've finally overcome
my deepest fears

About the Author

Kristin Michelle Elizabeth is a modern woman with an old soul, a non-traditional free spirit who lives by the notion of endless possibility and is on a constant quest for wisdom. She takes pain and fuels it to her creative advantage. She knows in order to achieve her greatest expression she must embrace her demons. A woman with many hats: creative, writer, poet, musician, and techie. She resides in eclectic Los Angeles, California.

You can find her on the web at kristinmichelleelizabeth.com.

"The courage to be yourself in a world constantly trying to shape you is my personal definition of power."

YOU MIGHT ALSO LIKE:

Your Soul is a River
by Nikita Gill

Bloom
by Shani Jay

Seeds Planted in Concrete
by Author Name

THOUGHT
CATALOG
Books

Made in the USA
San Bernardino, CA
03 October 2017